Developing Literacy
TEXT LEVEL

TEXT-LEVEL ACTIVITIES FOR THE LITERACY HOUR

year

Ray Barker

Christine Moorcroft

A & C BLACK

Reprinted 2000, 2001, 2002 (twice)
Published 2000 by
A&C Black Publishers Limited
37 Soho Square, London W1D 3QZ
www.acblack.com

ISBN 0-7136-5316-7

Acknowledgements
The authors and publishers are grateful for permission to reproduce the following:
page 10: cover illustrations from *Can't You Sleep, Little Bear?* © 1988 Barbara Firth,
written by Martin Waddell. Reproduced by permission of the publisher, Walker Books Ltd., London;
Rosie's Walk © Pat Hutchins, published by Bodley Head.
page 45: *Teddybears Eat Out* © Susanna Gretz and Alison Sage, published by A & C Black;
cover illustration from *This is the Bear* © 1986 Helen Craig, written by Sarah Hayes.
Reproduced by permission of the publisher, Walker Books Ltd., London;
Oscar Got the Blame © 1987 by Tony Ross, published by Andersen Press, London.

The authors and publishers would like to thank the following teachers
for their advice in producing this series of books:
Jane Beynon; Hardip Channa; Ann Hart; Lydia Hunt;
Rita Leader; Madeleine Madden; Helen Mason; Kim Pérez;
Joanne Turpin; Fleur Whatley

A CIP catalogue record for this book is
available from the British Library.

A & C Black uses paper produced with elemental chlorine-free pulp,
harvested from managed sustainable forests.

Printed in Great Britain by
St Edmundsbury Press Ltd, Bury St Edmunds, Suffolk.

Contents

Introduction

Developing Literacy: Text Level supports the teaching of reading and writing by providing a series of activities to develop children's ability to recognise and appreciate the different genres, styles and purposes of a variety of texts. **Year 1** develops the children's enjoyment of different kinds of rhymes and stories; it encourages them to notice repeated patterns and to predict the events in a story. **Year 1** also helps the children to compose their own stories and rhymes by encouraging them to notice the structures of those which they read and by providing frameworks on which they can create their own. It develops their ability to decide what they want to find out and how to use information books to find it, and it provides structures on which they can base their own non-fiction writing for particular purposes.

The children learn about different kinds of text, including stories with familiar settings and predictable and repeating patterns, fairy tales, stories and rhymes from different cultures, action rhymes and simple poems. They develop skills in planning and writing stories and poems; they read non-fiction texts such as signs, labels, captions, lists, instructions, information books and dictionaries. They learn how to plan and write their own non-fiction texts, including simple non-chronological reports.

The activities are designed to be carried out in the time allocated to independent work during the Literacy Hour. They support the objectives of the National Literacy Strategy *Framework for Teaching* at text level and they incorporate strategies which encourage independent learning – for example, ways in which children can check their own work or that of a partner. For the younger children, however, it is assumed that an adult will read the instructions with them. Investigation is given greater emphasis as the series progresses towards **Year 6**.

Year 1 helps children to develop skills to:

- read and write fiction and poetry through shared reading and writing;
- re-tell stories, giving the main points;
- write about familiar experiences linked with stories they read;
- identify the key issues of stories they read and to plan them in stories they write;
- explain why key events in stories happen;
- identify and use key features of story language;
- discuss characters in fiction and to create characters;
- identify basic story elements (beginning, middle and ending) and to use them in planning their own stories:
- use poems and rhymes they read as structures on which to write their own, for example, by substituting words.

Year 1 also develops the children's ability to:

- read and write non-fiction through shared reading and writing;
- read and write captions and labels;
- read, follow and write simple instructions;
- write lists for familiar purposes;
- differentiate between fiction and non-fiction books;
- use non-fiction books to find specific information and to answer questions;
- write simple questions;
- use dictionaries, glossaries and indexes;
- find out information from diagrams and charts, and to use them for recording and presenting information;
- plan their non-fiction writing;
- read recounts and recognise a sequence of events.

Extension

Most of the activity sheets end with a challenge (**Now try this!**) which reinforces and extends the children's learning and provides the teacher with an opportunity for assessment. These more challenging activities might be appropriate for only a few children; it is not expected that the whole class should complete them. On some pages there is space for the children to complete the extension activities, but for others the children will require a notebook or separate sheet of paper.

Organisation

Few resources are needed besides scissors, glue, word-banks, reference books and a range of simple dictionaries. Several activities are based on well-known stories and poems which the children need to have read, and to which they need access, but the activities have all been designed for use in conjunction either with readily available texts, or with texts of your choice.

To help teachers to select appropriate learning experiences for their pupils, the activities are grouped into sections within each book. The pages need not be presented in the order in which they appear in the books, unless otherwise stated.

Teachers' notes

Brief notes are provided at the bottom of most pages. They give ideas and suggestions for making the most of the activity sheet. They sometimes make suggestions for the whole class introduction, the plenary session or, possibly, for follow-up work using an adapted version of the activity sheet.

Structure of the Literacy Hour

The following chart shows an example of the way in which an activity from this book can be used to achieve the required organisation of the Literacy Hour.

Guess who: story characters (page 21)

Whole class introduction	15 min

Describe a story character and ask the children to guess who it is, for example: 'She wears a red cloak with a hood and she carries a basket'; 'It lives under a bridge and does not like people to cross the bridge'; or 'She has very long, strong hair. She is locked in a tower and she loves a prince.'

Whole class activity	15 min

Describe a character by giving one small piece of information at a time (details such as what he, she or it wears, says and looks like), stopping to invite the children to guess who it is. The first to guess correctly describes a character in the same way for the others to identify. Ask them what helped them to work out the character.

Group work	20 min

In pairs, one child describes a character's appearance (from a picture in a book) without naming him, her or it, while their partner draws this character without seeing the original. When the picture is finished the two children compare it with the original picture.

Independent work	20 min

The others work independently in groups or pairs from **Guess who: story characters** (page 21, **Developing Literacy: Text Level Year 1**).

Whole class plenary session	10 min

The children who have drawn story characters display them for the others to identify. Those who have played **Guess who: story characters** tell the others the kinds of questions which helped them to identify the characters: for example, 'Is it an animal?', 'Is it male?', or 'Is it a toy?'

Using the activity sheets

Fiction and poetry: reading comprehension

In **What happens here?** (page 9) the children learn about one of the elements of a story – the main place in which it happens. Introduce the word 'setting' and, for each story the children read, ask them about its setting.

Story settings (page 10) focuses the children's attention on the settings of well-known stories. They could draw or paint pictures of the settings of other stories they know. Their pictures could contribute to an interactive 'story settings' display on which there are prompts such as 'Find a story set at a farm' and 'Write the titles of two stories set in castles'.

David's new school (page 11) is a story which the children can relate to their own experience. Other stories about familiar experiences include: *Cleversticks* (Bernard Ashley, Collins), *The Magical Bicycle* (Berlie Doherty, Collins), *Can't You Sleep, Little Bear?* (Martin Waddell, Walker) and *Time for Bed* (Alexis Obi, Tamarind). The story on the activity sheet is an example of a story with a predictable pattern – a list of things which worry a little boy going into a school. The children could also predict a happy ending for the story.

The Three Little Pigs (page 12) is about patterned language in a story which the children can join in with during shared reading. They should notice the repetition of the words spoken by the wolf and of the outcome ('...And he did'), but they should also notice that the outcome of the final event is different (the wolf could not blow down the brick house).

Character mask (page 13) helps the children to notice the differences between written and spoken forms of a story. They could use the mask as a pattern to help them to make masks of other story characters which can be used while they re-tell stories. They could begin with words such as 'Hello. I'm the bear who…'

The Wheels on the Bus (page 14) is an example of a rhyme with a repeated pattern. It develops the children's ability to recognise repeated patterns in poems and rhymes and helps them to model their own writing.

Stories I like (page 15) introduces the idea that stories can be grouped according to type, for example: scary, funny, fairy tales, stories about trains, stories about children and animal stories. When naming a story they like, the children should be encouraged to justify their choice by naming one thing which they like about the story (for example, they might like a character, or they might like the jokes in a story).

In **The story of Noah** (page 16) the children are presented with the main events in a well-known story and asked to place them in the correct order. You could discuss other stories which the children know and ask them to describe the main events which happen in them, introducing the terms 'main' and 'event'. Write a brief summary of each event in a story, mix them up and invite the children to sequence them. Discuss the difficulties of telling a story if the events are in the wrong order.

Important events in a story (page 17) provides a format to help the children summarise the significant events in *any* story.

Why did it happen? (page 18) develops the children's ability to identify the causes of events in stories by answering questions which begin 'Why…?' or 'What made …?' Sometimes, one question raises another.

Story themes (page 19) is about common themes in stories. It will be useful (for the first activity) to have available copies of books such as *Cinderella*, *The Magic Porridge Pot* and *The Wizard of Oz*. For the second activity, useful stories include *The Pancake* and *The Gingerbread Man*.

Story words (page 20) is about the kinds of words and phrases which are often used in children's stories. This activity develops the children's ability to recognise three that are very common. Others include 'one morning/afternoon/evening/night', 'all day/night', 'all summer/winter', 'at last', 'the next day', 'happily ever after' and 'from that day on'.

In **Guess who: story characters** (page 21) the children need to be able to ask and answer questions about story characters. This activity draws their attention to details of some characters' appearance and nature.

Who will help? (page 22) requires the children to consider the nature, rather than the appearance, of story characters and to think about the ways in which the characters' behaviour might be affected by recent events. (For example, Jack might not be able to help Little Bo Peep because he is recovering from his fall down the hill!)

What did they say? (page 23) helps the children to become aware of dialogue.

Beginning a story, Predicting, Middle of a story, What happens next? and **Ending a story** (pages 24–28) are activities that develop the children's understanding of story elements and encourage them to recognise and continue a recurring pattern in a story. These activities should be carried out in the order in which they are presented. **Beginning a story** also develops the children's understanding of how the beginning of a story sets the scene and introduces the main characters.

Fiction and poetry: writing composition

I can do it! (page 29) is designed to encourage the children to discuss and write about a personal experience. A useful story book on this theme to read as a shared text is *The Magical Bicycle* (Berlie Doherty, Collins). The children should discuss, draw and write about the setbacks and difficulties they faced while they were learning to do something difficult. Did they feel like giving up? What kept them trying? How did they feel when they finally succeeded?

Make a rhyme (page 30) provides an opportunity for the children to model their writing on a simple rhyme, turning an old rhyme into a modern one. This can be linked with word-level work on rhyming words and onset and rime.

In **Lift the flap** (page 31) the children plan a story around a character and things which can be hidden under flaps. When reading 'lift-the-flap' books with them, point out how the character gets from one flap to another, for example, he or she could be looking for something (but finding other things under the flaps), or meeting other characters during a walk. The children could also make up questions whose answers could be hidden under flaps.

Old Macdonald's zoo (page 32) provides an opportunity for the children to to learn to write rhymes by using a well-known rhyme as a model.

The fly-away kite (page 33) helps the children to plan a story as if it were a film, frame by frame. In each frame there is a clue as to what happens in the next one. They should include this kind of clue in their own pictures.

The enchanted wood (page 34) provides a 'story map' which helps the children to plan a 'journey' story by using pictures and captions to represent the main events of a story. They are encouraged to imagine what or whom the character might encounter in each place and what he or she might do there.

Story wheels (page 35) encourages the children to use 'story language' in their own writing. The story wheel provides a starting point for their writing by helping them to create a character and a setting. Before this activity, it will be useful to have read shared texts and discussed their settings and characters.

A story character (page 36) can be used in conjunction with any story the children are reading and provides a structure on which to describe a character.

A special visitor (page 37) develops the children's ability to identify features of a character's nature from the way in which he or she behaves in the story. Using their understanding of a familiar story character, the children predict how he or she will behave in another situation.

Jason's problem (page 38) provides a model for the children to use as a structure on which to base their own stories. It can be used in conjunction with shared texts in which problems arise and are solved.

My own story setting (page 39) helps the children to build up the setting for a story by adding details.

My own counting poem (page 40) provides a model on which the children can write a counting poem which has a pattern but no rhyme. Teachers should read the prompts in the speech bubbles with the children. On different days they could take turns to read the first verse of their counting poem to the class; the others join in and continue the poem.

Jelly on the plate (page 41) uses a well-known verse as a model for the children's own verses which have rhythm, pattern and repetition. They should notice which lines are repeated, how often and where. This activity can be linked with word-level work on vowel sounds: making up new words by changing one vowel.

Line-finder (page 42) provides a selection of lines which can be used for making up verses with a similar pattern to those on page 41.

Non-fiction: reading comprehension

Signs in the park (page 43) is about reading and using captions. It can be linked with work in geography lessons using pictorial maps.

Job list (page 44) develops the children's ability to read and follow simple instructions.

Fiction or non-fiction? (page 45) develops the children's ability to distinguish between fiction and non-fiction books by looking at their covers. They could sort a collection of books from the class library into 'fiction' and 'non-fiction' sets.

Choose a book (page 46) helps children learn that non-fiction books can be used to answer questions.

The contents page (page 47) shows the children how to use the contents page of a non-fiction book for deciding which pages they need to read. It helps them to understand that non-fiction books need not be read from beginning to end, page by page.

The glossary (page 48) encourages the children to use the glossary of a non-fiction book to find the meanings of new words.

Dictionary (page 49) encourages the children use a dictionary to check the spellings of words once they have tried to spell them for themselves and develops their understanding of alphabetical order.

The index (page 50) helps the children to use the index of a non-fiction book; it shows them that an index is arranged in alphabetical order but that not every letter of the alphabet might be needed, depending on the items indexed.

Information books (page 51) encourages the children to use more than one information book to find out what they need to know; it helps them to realise that different information books about the same subject give differing information.

Planting seeds (page 52) develops the children's understanding of recounts; they learn that a recount has to be written in the order of what happened and they use some of the language of chronological reports.

Non-fiction: writing composition

Fruits (page 53) develops the children's ability to gather information from diagrams.

Writing captions (page 54) helps the children to write extended captions, which give more information than headings. They could also write captions which explain pictures they have drawn or to describe class displays.

Writing a list (page 55) provides a vertical format for a list, with pictorial prompts.

Writing a plan (page 56) provides a vertical format for a list of things to do as well as practice in gathering information from labelled pictures. It also revises the use of labels. The children can use this format when planning work in design technology.

Writing instructions: 1 (page 57) provides a picture prompt, together with a word-bank, to help the children to write simple rules for using dressing-up clothes. The children could also help to write rules for using equipment in their own classroom.

Writing instructions: 2 (page 58) provides prompts and a word-bank which help the children to write instructions for making a model, step by step. It can be linked with work in art, design technology and information and communications technology.

Writing questions (page 59) provides a structure for using reference books: the children decide what they want to find out and write it in the form of questions.

Making a chart: 1 (page 60) shows the children one way in which to organise the information they have found out from reference books (or ICT sources or practical work). This page could be used in connection with work in science on the properties of materials.

Making a chart: 2 (page 61) provides a format for a simple comparison chart which is especially useful in history lessons.

Beach report (page 62) is about the writing of simple non-chronological reports. To help the children, the sentences are started for them and a word-bank is provided.

Writing a factfile (page 63) is about presenting information in a simple way which does not require sentences. The children could also store factfiles using computer software. Factfiles from the whole class could be combined to form a database about animals.

Planning a non-fiction book (page 64) provides a structure for planning a simple non-fiction book. It helps the children to organise the contents of the book into separate pages.

Glossary of terms used

genre A specific type of writing or other medium of communication, for example: legend, newspaper story or poem.
non-chronological writing Writing organised without reference to any time sequence. It is usually organised by attributes, for example: writing about the children's own school could be organised into grounds, building, teachers and children.
onomatopoeia The use of words which echo sounds associated with their meaning, for example: *bang, boom, squeak*.
phoneme The smallest unit of sound in a word. A phoneme can be represented by one to four letters, for example: b<u>a</u>t, s<u>tay</u>, st<u>ripe</u>, <u>eight</u>.
recount A text (or part of a text) written to describe an event or series of events for information or entertainment. It uses descriptive language and might include dialogue. It is usually written in the past tense.
report A non-chronological text written to describe or classify. It is usually written in the present tense.
rime The part of a syllable which contains the vowel and final consonant or consonant cluster, if there is one, for example; c<u>at</u>, c<u>ow</u>.

What happens here?

Which story takes place in this setting?

- **Write the title.**

_____

- **Draw what happens.**

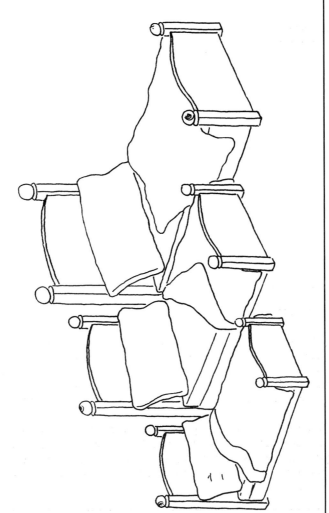

- **Write about what happened in your picture.**

Teachers' note The children need to have listened to, or read, _Goldilocks and the Three Bears_ (but not immediately before beginning the activity). As a guided writing activity, help the children to create (by drawing and describing) a setting for their own story.

Developing Literacy
Text Level Year 1
© A & C Black

Story settings

- **Join the story titles to the settings.**

Titles

Hansel and Gretel

The Three Billy Goats Gruff

Can't You Sleep, Little Bear?

Rosie's Walk

Settings

Now try this!

- **Draw three other story settings.**
- **Write each title on a piece of paper.**
- **Give them to a partner to match.**

Teachers' note To introduce this activity, hold up a story book which the children know and ask them where the story takes place using the term 'setting'. It would be useful to have access to the stories shown on this page as well as other stories which they know.

Developing Literacy
Text Level Year 1
© A & C Black

David's new school

- **Read the story.**
- **Draw two other pictures about David's school.**
- **Write the words.**

David was in a new school.
He didn't know where to sit.

David didn't know where to hang his coat.

David didn't know _____

_____

_____

_____

David didn't know _____

_____

_____

_____

What else worries David?

- **Draw a picture and write the words.**

Teachers' note You could introduce the activity by talking about how it feels to move into a new school. Read the first two sentences of the story with the children and ask them what else they think might bother David because he doesn't know about it.

Developing Literacy
Text Level Year 1
© A & C Black

The Three Little Pigs

- **Read the story.**

- **Write the missing words.**

I have built my house out of straw.

I'll huff and I'll puff, And I'll blow your house down.

...And he did!

I have built my house out of wood.

I'll huff and I'll puff, And I'll blow your house down.

...And he did!

I have built my house out of bricks.

_____

_____

_____

_____

Now try this!

- **Did the wolf blow down the brick house?**

- **Write a sentence about what happened.**

- **Draw a picture.**

Teachers' note To introduce the activity, you could read the story of *The Three Little Pigs* as a shared text, stopping at the repeated words so that the children can supply them. Draw their attention to the difference between the outcome of the wolf's attempts to blow down the straw and wooden houses and the brick house.

Developing Literacy
Text Level Year 1
© A & C Black

Character mask

Teachers' note Copy this page on to card. The children can colour and cut out the mask and then glue it on to a lollipop stick. In pairs or in a group, the children could re-tell a story about a bear or make up their own stories enacting the part of a bear. They could pretend to have a teddy bears' picnic.

Developing Literacy
Text Level Year 1
© A & C Black

The Wheels on the Bus

- **Read the rhyme.**

The wheels on the bus go round and round,

Round and round, round and round.

The wheels on the bus go round and round,

All day long.

on the bus goes toot toot toot,

- **Write other words
  in the gaps.**

The _____ on the bus goes toot toot toot,

The _____ , _____ ,

The _____ on the bus goes _____ ,

All day long.

- **Write a verse about a dog on the bus.**

Developing Literacy
Text Level Year 1

Teachers' note Read the first verse as a shared text and then encourage the children to join in and complete other verses orally, for example: 'The people on the bus go …', and 'The wipers on the bus go …'

Stories I like

- **Tick the kinds of stories you like.** ✓

scary stories ☐	fairy tales ☐
funny stories ☐	
stories about trains ☐	stories about children ☐
	animal stories ☐

Books shown: Spooks, What's that Noise?, Mr Funny, Prince Cinders, Hansel and Gretel, Sleeping Beauty, The Train Ride, Thomas the Tank Engine, Alfie's Feet, Titch, Farmer Duck, The Little Red Hen

- **Fill in the chart about a story you like.**

Title	Type of story	What I like in the story

- **Make a chart about another story you like.**

Now try this!

Teachers' note You could write each type of story on a card and introduce the activity by showing the children a collection of stories of the types shown. Ask the children to indicate which card belongs to each story.

Developing Literacy
Text Level Year 1
© A & C Black

The story of Noah

• **Cut out the pictures.**

There will be a big flood. You must build an ark, Noah.

• **Put the pictures in order.**

• **Tell the story with a partner.**

Now try this!

• **Draw the next event in the story.**

Teachers' note This sheet supports collaborative story telling. Read the story of Noah as a shared text either from a children's Bible or from *Noah's Ark* (Lucy Cousins, Walker). The children could re-tell other stories they know by drawing pictures (and giving them captions – an adult transcribing if necessary) of the main events.

Developing Literacy
Text Level Year 1
© A & C Black

Important events in a story

- **Write the title of the story.**

_____

- **What happens in the story?**
- **Write and draw the main things.**

What happens	Picture
1. _____ _____ _____	
2. _____ _____ _____	
3. _____ _____ _____	
4. _____ _____ _____	

Teachers' note This activity sheet can be used with any story the children read independently, during guided reading or as a shared text. They might not need to use all the boxes, or they might need extra boxes in which to write.

Developing Literacy
Text Level Year 1
© **A & C Black**

Why did it happen?

- **Write what happened.**

Why was Jack's mum angry?

Word-bank

beans   cow

Jack swapped the

_____ for a bag

of _____.

Why did a beanstalk grow in Jack's garden?

Word-bank

beans   threw   window

Jack's mum _____ his

_____ out of the

_____ because she

was angry.

Now try this!

- **Draw an event from another story.**

- **Why did it happen?**

Write a sentence.

Teachers' note The children need to have read, and have access to, a copy of *Jack and the Beanstalk*. Before the extension activity, you could discuss with the children any book they have read recently and ask them what made a particular event in it happen.

Developing Literacy
Text Level Year 1
© A & C Black

Story themes

- **Write the titles of three stories with magic spells in them.**

- **Write the titles of two stories about a chase.**

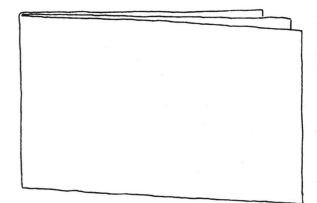

- **Sort some story books into sets with the same theme.**
- **Label each set.**

Work with a friend.

Teachers' note Introduce the term 'theme' and hold up a copy of a story which involves magic, for example, *Sleeping Beauty*. Ask the children what the magic spell did. Show them a collection of other story books and ask them if any of them are about magic spells. For the extension activity, provide a collection of story books for the children to sort.

Developing Literacy
Text Level Year 1
© A & C Black

Story words

• **Read these parts of stories.**

• **Fill in the gaps.**

_____

there was a little red hen.

She _____ in a little

house. _____

the little red hen found

some grains of wheat.

Country Mouse _____ in the country.

Town Mouse _____ in the town.

_____ Town Mouse

went to stay in the country.

_____ there was a poor

woman who _____ with her little girl.

_____ they had nothing

left to eat.

• **Write some other words which are often**

used in stories.

Teachers' note Before the activity, encourage the children to identify the 'story words' in the word-bank in other books they read. Begin collecting other examples of 'story words'. On photocopied sections of stories, the children could also underline examples of 'story words'.

Developing Literacy
Text Level Year 1
© A & C Black

Guess who: story characters

The Genie	Puss-in-Boots	Sleeping Beauty
Pinocchio	Aladdin	The Little Red Hen
Little Red Riding Hood	Hansel	The Wicked Queen
Rapunzel	Rumpelstiltskin	The Tin Man

Teachers' note Make two copies per group of children. Cut out the characters from one sheet. One child chooses a character and places it face down. Looking at the other sheet, the others try to find out who it is by asking questions which can only be answered by 'yes' or 'no'. They cover characters as they are eliminated. No guessing is allowed – characters have to be eliminated one by one.

Developing Literacy
Text Level Year 1
© A & C Black

Who will help?

Little Bo Peep has lost her sheep.

• Tick the characters who

might help her. ✓

Jack ☐

The Ugly Sisters ☐

The Wolf ☐

Dorothy ☐

Snow White ☐

Hansel ☐

The Wicked Queen ☐

The Witch ☐

Now try this!

• Draw and write about two other fairy tale characters who might help Little Bo Peep.

Why do you think they might help her?

Teachers' note The children need to know the fairy tale and nursery rhymes srepresented by characters on the page. You could ask them to explain how they know if a character might help. Before the extension activity, discuss other fairy tale characters which the children know.

Developing Literacy
Text Level Year 1
© A & C Black

• **Read this page from The Little Red Hen.**

> The Little Red Hen asked, 'Who will help me to plant these seeds?'
> 'Not I,' said the goose.
> 'Not I,' said the cat.
> 'Not I,' said the pig.
> 'Then I'll plant them myself,' said the Little Red Hen.

What did each character say?

• **Write the words.**

What happened next?

• **Draw the animals.**

• **Write what they said.**

Teachers' note This activity can be adapted to work with dialogues from any story read as a shared text. Groups of children could also make character puppets with which to enact the story.

Developing Literacy
Text Level Year 1
© A & C Black

Beginning a story

Here is the beginning of a story called Hide and Seek. It tells you about the setting and the characters.

It is raining.
Susie and Sam have to stay indoors.

The setting	The characters
Susie and Sam's house.	Susie Sam

- **Read the beginning of another book.**
- **Draw and write on the chart.**

The setting	The characters
_____	_____
_____	_____
_____	_____

Teachers' note When reading any story with the children, ask them what the beginning of the story tells them. You could make a display of 'story beginnings' on to which the children could fix information about the settings and characters of the stories.

Developing Literacy
Text Level Year 1
© A & C Black

Predicting

- ## Here is some more of Hide and Seek.

'We can't play in the garden,'
says Sam.
'We'll have to play indoors,'
says Susie.
'What shall we play?'
asks Sam.

- ## Tick what you think they play.

Snakes and
ladders ☐

Hide and
seek ☐

Computer
games ☐

- ## Why do you think this? _____

_____

Now
try
this!

- ## Read the beginning of another story.

What do you think will happen?

- ## Draw and write about it.

Teachers' note The children should first complete page 24. Explain that this page continues the
story *Hide and Seek*. Read the extract with the children and ask them what they think will happen.
What makes them think that? (They should consider the title of the book.)

Developing Literacy
Text Level Year 1
© A & C Black

Middle of a story

Here is some more of Hide and Seek.

'Let's play hide and seek,'
says Susie.
Sam begins to count to ten.
Susie looks for a place to hide.

One...
...two...

She can't
hide here.

It's too smelly.

...three...
...four...

She can't
hide here.

It's too small.

...five...
...six...

She can't
hide here.

It's too wet.

Where can Susie try next?

• Draw and write.

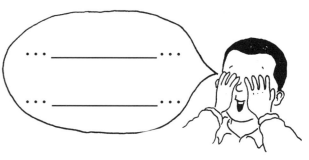

She can't _____

_____

It's too

_____

Teachers' note The children should first complete pages 24 and 25. Explain that this page continues the story *Hide and Seek*. Read the extract with the children, ask them where Susie might try to hide next and what numbers Sam will count. Will she be able to hide there? What stops it being a good hiding place?

Developing Literacy
Text Level Year 1
© A & C Black

26

What happens next?

Here is a bit more of Hide and Seek.

Nine...TEN! I'm coming to find you.

She's not under here.

She's not behind this.

She's not in here.

- **Write what Sam says.**

- **Draw where Sam looks next.**
- **Write what he says.**

She's not _____ _____

_____ _____

Teachers' note The children should first complete pages 24–26. Ask the children where they think Sam will look next and whether he will find Susie.

**Developing Literacy
Text Level Year 1
© A & C Black**

Ending a story

This is what happens near the end of Hide and Seek.

Where is Susie hiding?

What is it like there?

• **Draw and write.**

_____

_____

_____

Teachers' note The children should first complete pages 24–27. Explain that this is the ending of *Hide and Seek*. Before introducing the activity, ask the children, 'Did Sam find Susie? Where might Susie be hiding? Is it a good hiding place? Is this the end of the story? Do you think it could be continued?' (They might suggest that it is Sam's turn to hide.)

Developing Literacy
Text Level Year 1
© A & C Black

I can do it!

Asma had a new bike. She tried and tried to ride it. But she fell off every time.

Her mum held the bike. But every time she let go, Asma fell off.

• Draw and write about something you could not do.

Trying hard

_____

_____

_____

_____

Trying again

_____

_____

_____

_____

 **• Write about how you felt when you <u>could</u> do it.**

Draw a picture.

Teachers' note You could discuss things the children have learned to do but which have not been easy, for example: riding a bike, roller-skating, swimming and catching a ball. Ask them how they felt when they were trying to do it, when they watched other people who could do it and when they succeeded.

Developing Literacy
Text Level Year 1
© A & C Black

Make a rhyme

I had a dog whose name was Fred.

I sent him to market for a basket of bread.

- **Complete the verses.**

- **Draw pictures.**

I had a dog whose name was Sam.

I sent him to market for a jar of _____ .

Sam

I had a dog whose name was Sunny.

I sent him to market for a _____ .

- **Write two other verses.**

These words might help you.

| cake | ham | jelly | meat | pie | tea |

Teachers' note Read the verse aloud with the children, stressing the words which rhyme. During the plenary session, they could take turns to read their verses, stopping before the word which rhymes with the dog's name so that the others can supply it. Their verses could be pasted into a scrapbook to form a class poem.

Developing Literacy
Text Level Year 1
© A & C Black

Lift the flap

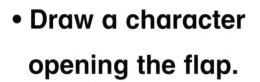

- **Cut out the flap.**

- **Fold it back.**

- **Draw a character opening the flap.**

- **Draw something to go under the flap.**

Glue your picture underneath the flap.

- **Make three other lift-the-flap pages.**

- **Draw characters opening the flaps.**

- **Glue a different picture under each flap.**

- **Write the story.**

Teachers' note Read some 'lift-the-flap' books with the children; ask them to predict what is under each flap. They need four copies of this page on which to draw the scenes in their story. Under the flaps there might be something for which the character is looking, something he or she comes across during a walk, or a surprise.

Developing Literacy
Text Level Year 1
© A & C Black

Old Macdonald's zoo

- **Read the song.**

- **Fill in the gaps.**

Old Macdonald had a zoo,

Ee aye ee aye oh!

And in that zoo he had some tigers.

Ee aye ee aye oh!

With a grrr, grrr here,

And a _____ , _____ there.

Old Macdonald had a zoo,

Ee aye ee aye oh!

And in that zoo he had some snakes.

Ee _____ !

With a _____ , _____ here,

And a _____ , _____ there.

- **Write verses about these animals.**

parrots   dolphins   monkeys

Teachers' note Begin with the well-known rhyme *Old Macdonald had a Farm* and ask the children how a zoo is different. Ask them to make the noise of each animal and then try to write it (encourage them to sound out all the phonemes).

Developing Literacy
Text Level Year 1
© A & C Black

The fly-away kite

• **Finish the picture story.**

 • **Cut out the pictures.**

• **Glue them into a book.**

• **Write the story.**

Teachers' note You could enlarge this page and use it as a shared text. To introduce the activity, cover all but the first picture and ask the children to look at it carefully and predict what might happen; reveal the second picture and discuss and refine their predictions before revealing the third. What might happen next?

Developing Literacy
Text Level Year 1
© **A & C Black**

The enchanted wood

- **Take a story character for a walk through the enchanted wood.**
- **Write what happens in the boxes.**

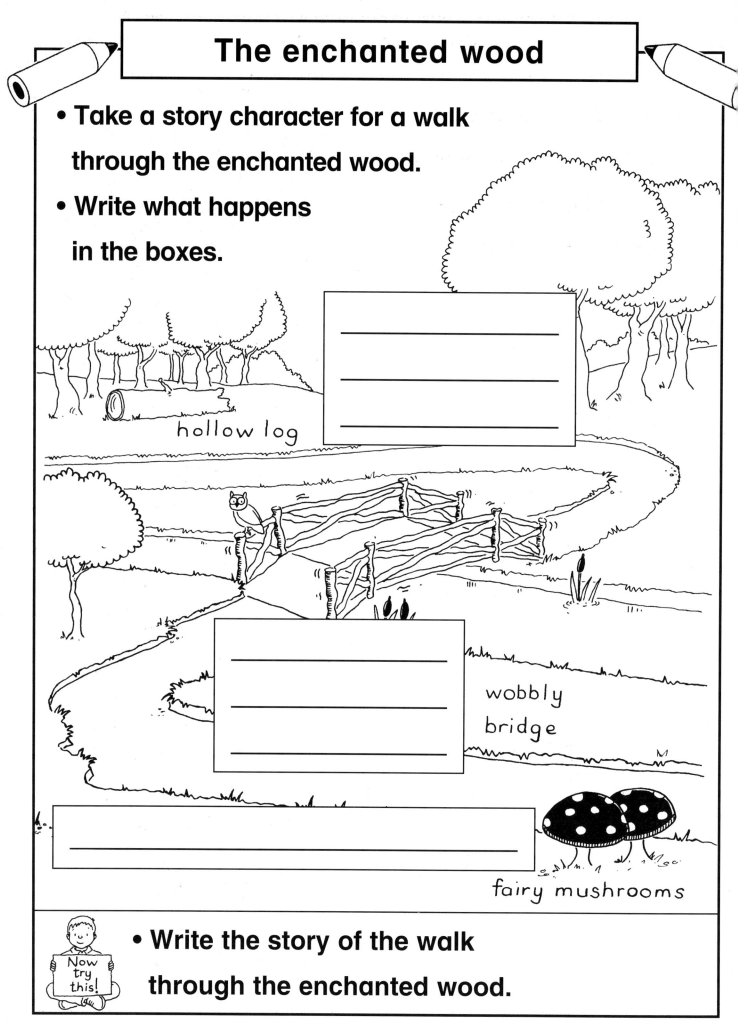

hollow log

wobbly bridge

fairy mushrooms

- **Write the story of the walk through the enchanted wood.**

Now try this!

Teachers' note The children could take a model character for a walk through the enchanted wood, telling a partner what happens in each place. In the boxes they write notes about what happens, so that the sheet forms a story plan.

Developing Literacy
Text Level Year 1
© A & C Black

Story wheels

- **Cut out the wheels.**

- **Put the small wheel on top of the large wheel.**

- **Join them in the middle with a paper fastener.**

lived in a little cottage.

lived in an old boot.

lived in a golden palace.

lived in a hollow log.

lived in a cave.

lived on top of a hill.

A beautiful princess

A happy mouse

A kind old bear

A wicked old woman

A little pink pig

A terrible troll

Teachers' note In groups of two to four, the children take turns to choose a character and a setting by turning the wheel. They tell the others about the character's lifestyle (and family, if relevant). They could talk about a 'big event' (perhaps a problem or something funny) which happens ('One day...'), and the outcome of this event. The children could then write their stories.

Developing Literacy
Text Level Year 1
© A & C Black

A story character

• **Write a story character's name.**

_____

Draw a picture of the character.

• **What is the character like?** _____

_____

• **Write how you know.** _____

_____

_____

_____

_____

What would the character do in your classroom?

• **Draw and write about it.**

Now try this!

Teachers' note This can be used with a story used during shared or guided reading. Talk about the characters in the story and ask the children to give words to describe them. Ask what the character has done or said which shows what he or she is like.

Developing Literacy
Text Level Year 1
© A & C Black

A special visitor

- **Imagine that a story character is visiting your home.**
- **Draw and write.**

Think about what makes him or her happy.

Character's name _____

What shall I give him or her to eat?

_____

_____

_____

What shall we do?

_____

_____

_____

Now try this!

- **Where will the story character sleep?**

Draw and write.

Teachers' note Ask the children which story character they would like to invite to their home. Discuss the foods the character likes (if they know) and, if not, what they think he or she might like (and what makes them think this). Similarly, discuss what the character likes to do.

Developing Literacy
Text Level Year 1
© A & C Black

Jason's problem

Jason has some new paints.
'I'm going to paint a
picture of you, Sooty,'
he says to his cat.
Sooty sits on the table.

 Jason has a problem.   But then...

There is no black
paint left.

Sooty finds a pot of paint
in Jason's bedroom.

• Draw and write about another problem for Jason.

_____   _____

_____   _____

_____   _____

Now try this!

• Write the rest of the story.

Teachers' note Read the story with the children and ask them what problem Jason had and how it was solved. The children could suggest other problems which might happen, for example, Sooty knocks the water over, or the paint is too wet and runs down the picture. They then suggest solutions to the problems and, finally, a happy ending.

Developing Literacy
Text Level Year 1
© A & C Black

My own story setting

- **Geeta is planning a setting for a story.**

The setting is a beach.

There is a cave in the cliffs.

In the cave there is a big box.

- **Choose one of these story settings.**

| a forest |
| an old house |
| a river bank |

- **Draw it.**

Add things to the setting, as I did.

- **Write the rest of the story.**

Now try this!

Teachers' note Before the activity, show the children a very simple picture of a story setting (you could use a big book page or a poster with a clear plastic overlay on which the children can draw). Ask them to add other things to the setting; as the setting is built up, the children should be able to suggest events which might happen there.

Developing Literacy
Text Level Year 1
© A & C Black

My own counting poem

Ten little sausages,
Sizzling in the pan.
One got eaten –
And then there were nine.

• **Write the next verse.**

Nine _____

_____

_____

_____

• **Write your own counting poem.**

Ten little _____

What were they?

What were they doing?

Where?

_____

_____

What happened?

_____

How many were left?

• **Start the next verse.**

_____

Now try this!

• **Finish the poem by saying it with a partner.**

Teachers' note Read the first verse with the children and encourage them to supply the second verse, and so on until the line, 'And then there were none,' is reached. Model example verses with the children, for example: 'Ten little shirts hanging on the line/One blew away...', 'Ten little cars parked in the road/One drove away/And then there were nine.'

Developing Literacy
Text Level Year 1
© A & C Black

40

Jelly on the plate

Jelly on the plate,
Jelly on the plate.
Wibble, wobble,
Wibble, wobble,
Jelly on the plate.

• **Fill in the gaps in this verse.**

Water in the glass,
Water _____
_____
_____
Water in the glass.

• **Write another verse.**

Crisps _____
_____
_____
_____
_____ .

 • **Write a verse about one of these foods.**

| soup | apples | spaghetti |

Teachers' note Model some examples with the children and write them on the board or a flip-chart (page 42 provides some ideas), pointing out the pattern of the verse by asking questions: 'What is the food?', 'What is it in or on?', 'What does it do?'

Developing Literacy
Text Level Year 1
© A & C Black

Line-finder

Cream in a jug	Glug, glog
Pancake in the air	Flip, flap
Beans on toast	Squish, squash
Cake on a plate	Crimble, crumble
Sausage in the pan	Sizzle, sazzle
Noodles in a wok	Crickle, crackle
Lolly on a stick	Drip, drop
Naan in the oven	Piff, puff

Teachers' note (For use with page 41). You could photocopy the page on to card and laminate it for re-use before cutting out the cards. Mix them up and give them to the children. Ask the children to match the foods with their sounds, then to use the cards to make up their own verses which have the same pattern as *Jelly on the plate*.

Developing Literacy
Text Level Year 1
© A & C Black

Signs in the park

- **Read the labels on the park plan.**

- **Write the words on the signposts.**

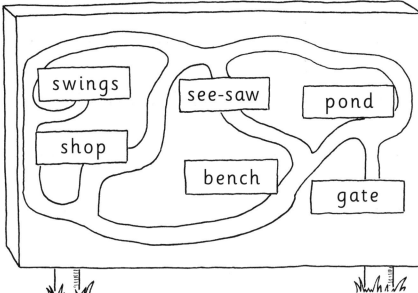

Park plan

swings
see-saw
pond
shop
bench
gate

- **Draw a plan of a garden.**

- **Write labels on your plan.**

Teachers' note Help the children to read the plan and to relate it to the picture of the park. The extension activity could be adapted by providing gardening magazines and garden centre brochures from which the children can cut pictures to fix on to a collage which they then label.

The children are planning a party.

- **Read what they say.**

Simon	Faye	Laura
Harry	Tariq	Jane

- **Write the children's names on the job list.**

balloons _____

cakes _____

goody bags _____

invitations _____

shopping _____

table _____

Now try this!

- **Draw six children planning a picnic.**
- **Write their job list.**

rs' note Following the extension activity, the children could arrange the listed jobs in the
 ...hich they need to be done. They could also write job lists for their own groups for
 ...k in other lessons.

Fiction or non-fiction?

Teddybears
Eat Out

Susanna Gretz
Alison Sage

Toys

Peter Smith

Birds

Susan Ray

France

Bill Jones

This is the Bear

Sarah Hayes Helen Craig

Oscar Got the
Blame

Tony Ross

Cinderella

Picture
Dictionary

Children's
Recipes

Teachers' note Photocopy the page and cut out the book covers. In pairs the children sort them into two sets, 'fiction' and 'non-fiction'. They should discuss the covers and decide whether the books are giving information or telling a story, giving reasons.

Developing Literacy
Text Level Year 1
© A & C Black

Choose a book

- **Read the children's questions.**

- **Choose a book which will tell them the answers.**

 What do ladybirds eat?

 Mosques Rome

 How does a torch work?

Where is Rome?

 Dinosaurs

 Light

What does 'jest' mean?

 Insects

What did dinosaurs eat?

 Dictionary

 What is it like in a mosque?

 Now try this!

What would you like to know?

- **Write the question.** _____

_____

- **Choose a book to answer your question.**

- **Write the name of the book.**

_____

Teachers' note Before the children write their own question in the extension activity, discuss the topic within which they will ask the question (it could be linked with work in another subject) and ask them to write or say what they already know about the topic. Discuss the kinds of questions which can be answered using books.

Developing Literacy
Text Level Year 1
© A & C Black

The contents page

Which pages should the children read?

- **Write the page number in the box.**

How do muscles work?

How do we see things?

What gives skin its colour?

Contents

Bones	2	Eyes	12
Muscles	4	Ears	14
Skin	6	Glossary	15
Hair	8	Index	16
Teeth	10		

How many bones are there in my leg?

What does the ear-drum do?

What is hair made of?

- **Copy a question from this sheet.**
- **Find a book to help you to answer it.**

Write on the back of this sheet.

- **Which pages do you need to read?**

Teachers' note Read the questions with the children and model the first example with them. For the extension activity the children will need a reference book. Instead of a question from this page, the children could write a question on a topic about which they are learning in another subject.

Developing Literacy
Text Level Year 1
© A & C Black

The glossary

- **Read the pages.**

- **Which words need to be in the glossary?**

- **Underline the words.**

The builders make foundations for the house. They dig trenches. They fill the trenches with concrete.

The bricklayers build the walls. They put in frames for the doors and windows.

The builders make a frame for the roof. They put roofing felt on it.

Now try this!

- **Choose two of the glossary words.**

Use a dictionary.

- **Find out what they mean.**

Teachers' note To introduce the activity, read the first extract with the children and ask them to indicate the 'new' words. During the plenary session, discuss the meanings of the glossary words.

Developing Literacy
Text Level Year 1
© A & C Black

Dictionary

- **Write the captions.**
- **Check your spellings.**
- **Re-write the captions**
  if you need to.

Use a dictionary.

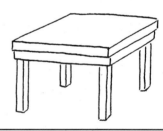

Now try this!

- **Think of two other words**
  that you cannot spell.
- **Try to spell them.**
- **Check them. Re-write them.**

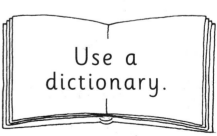

Use a dictionary.

Teachers' note It might be necessary to revise alphabetical order before carrying out this activity. Encourage the children to spell the words by sounding each phoneme and writing it in the way in which they *think* it should be written.

Developing Literacy
Text Level Year 1
© A & C Black

The index

These words are missing from the index.

tunnel	cliff	river	hill
bridge	wood	pond	lake

- ## Write the missing words in the index.

Index

b

beach   2, 3

_____   6

c

_____   3

h

_____   8, 9

l

_____   10

p

path   7

_____   11

r

_____   10, 11

road   6, 7

s

seashore   2, 3

stream   10, 11

t

_____   6, 11

w

waterfall   10, 11

_____

- ## Write these words in alphabetical order.

station	railway	garage	hotel	train

Teachers' note It might be necessary to revise alphabetical order before carrying out this activity.
Draw the children's attention to the alphabetical order of the index which they can use to help
them find an item, and to the numbers which show the page on which it appears.

Developing Literacy
Text Level Year 1
© A & C Black

Information books

- **Choose three books for each child.**

My topic is trains.

1 _____

2 _____

3 _____

My topic is plants.

1 _____

2 _____

3 _____

My topic is space.

1 _____

2 _____

3 _____

- **Choose three books for your own topic.**
- **Draw the covers and write the titles.**

Teachers' note Model the first example with the children: ask them to suggest words connected with trains (for example, railway, steam) before selecting the books. For the extension activity they should be given a topic (connected with work in another subject) about which to find information, and they will need reference books.

Developing Literacy
Text Level Year 1
© A & C Black

Planting seeds

- **Cut out the pictures.**

- **Put them in order.**

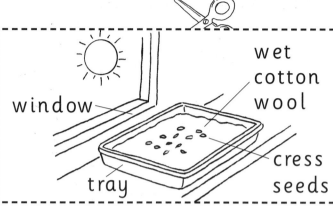

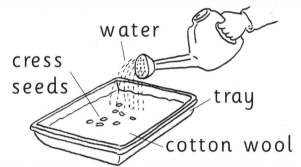

- **Cut out the captions.**

- **Put them beneath the pictures.**

- **Glue the pictures and words on to paper.**

Last of all I put the tray by the window.	First I put some cotton wool in a tray.
After that I watered the seeds.	Then I put some cress seeds on the cotton wool.

Teachers' note This activity could be used as a model on which to base the children's own recounts of work they have done in other subjects, such as science or mathematics.

Developing Literacy
Text Level Year 1
© A & C Black

Fruits

- **Look at the pictures.**
- **Read the words.**

kiwi

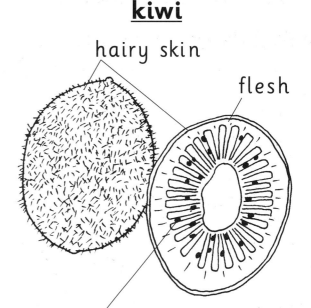

hairy skin

flesh

seeds

plum

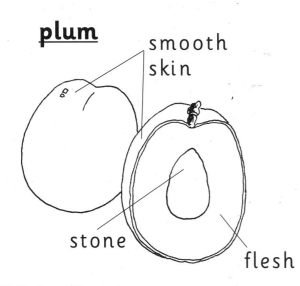

smooth skin

stone

flesh

- **Fill in the gaps.**

The plum has _____ skin.

The plum has one seed called a _____.

There is _____ around the stone.

The kiwi has _____ skin.

The kiwi has many _____.

There is _____ around the seeds.

Now try this!

- **Look at a diagram in another book.**
- **What does the diagram tell you?**
- **Write two sentences.**

Teachers' note Begin by reading a shared text in which there is a labelled diagram: ask the children to take turns to give a sentence about the item depicted. Before the children begin the extension activity, the term 'diagram' should be introduced.

Developing Literacy
Text Level Year 1
© A & C Black

Writing captions

• **Finish the caption for each picture.**

Alice has drawn a picture of a dog and _____

Word-bank

butterfly

cat

flowers

plane

ship

Paul has drawn a picture of

_____

_____

May _____

_____

_____

_____

• **Write a caption for a picture that you have drawn.**

Now try this!

Teachers' note Discuss the pictures and read the words in the word-bank with the children.

Developing Literacy
Text Level Year 1
© A & C Black

Writing a list

What does a new baby need?

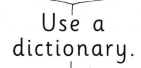
Use a dictionary.

• **Write a list.**

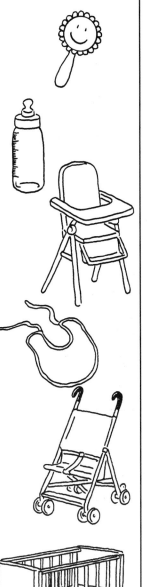

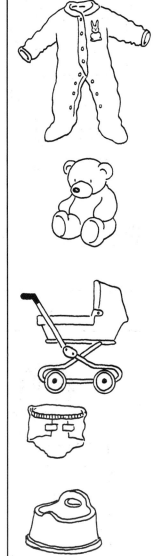

Now try this!

• **Write a list of five things a dog needs.**

Check your spellings.

Teachers' note You could introduce the activity by reading, as shared texts, shopping lists and lists of things to do. Encourage the children to spell the words by sounding each phoneme and to check them by using word-banks, dictionaries and catalogues of baby goods. Point out the shape of the list and that each item should be written on a new line.

Developing Literacy
Text Level Year 1
© A & C Black

Writing a plan

Balraj is going to make a model garden.

- **Write what he will do.**

paper
grass
twigs
mirror
stones
sand
saucer
paper
flowers

1. Put some sand in a saucer.

2. _____

3. _____

4. _____

5. _____

6. _____

- **Draw and write a plan for something you will make.**

Teachers' note Discuss the picture and ask the children what Balraj will need in order to make his garden. Read the first sentence with them and ask what Balraj should do next. (There is no 'right' order.) In the extension activity, the children could first draw a picture showing what they want to make.

**Developing Literacy
Text Level Year 1
© A & C Black**

Writing instructions: 1

The children's dressing-up clothes are in a mess!

- **Write some instructions to help the children tidy up.**

Word-bank

boots   box

clothes-rack

dresses

hang up

hangers   hats

shirts   shoes

trousers

Hang up the dresses.
_____

_____

_____

_____

_____

_____

Now try this!

- **Write three rules for using something in your classroom.**

Work with a partner.

Teachers' note During a guided writing session discuss the picture and ask the children what the children in the activity have done/not done. List their responses and, taking each item in turn, ask them to say what the children *should* and *should not* do.

Developing Literacy
Text Level Year 1
© A & C Black

• **First, make a model dog like this one.**

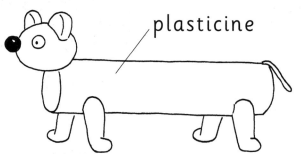

plasticine

• **Now complete the instructions to show how to make the dog.**

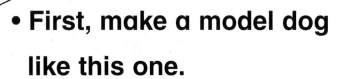

Word-bank

ball	board
four	little
plastic knife	press
roll	sausage
shape	squash
squeeze	two

You need

a board

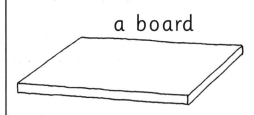

1. Make the body.

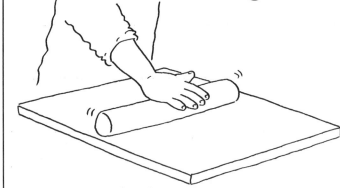

Roll some plasticine into a _____ shape.

• **Write and draw instructions for making**

| **2.** the head | **3.** the legs | **4.** the tail | **5.** the ears |

Teachers' note The children could make the plasticine model before the Literacy Hour.
Provide the equipment and use the words listed in the word-bank.

Developing Literacy
Text Level Year 1
© A & C Black

Writing questions

Here is a bee.

What would you like to know about bees?

• **Write some questions.**

Word-bank

How	What
Where	Why
buzz	
flowers	
fly	
honey	
queen	
sting	

What do bees eat?

_____

_____

_____

_____

_____

Now try this!

• **Write the answers to two of your questions.**

Use information books.

Teachers' note Provide reference books about bees and insects in general. To introduce the activity discuss the picture and ask the children what they know about bees; this might raise some questions.

Developing Literacy
Text Level Year 1
© A & C Black

Making charts: 1

- **Read the chart.**

- **Find out about these materials.**

Use information books.

  metal

 plastic

stone

glass

 wood

- **Fill in the chart.** ✓ or ✗

Material	Does it float?	Does it rust?	Does it bend?
glass			
metal			
plastic			
stone			
wood			

- **Find out which materials are used to make these things.**

 beakers and cups

 pans

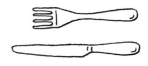 knives and forks

Teachers' note Provide reference books about materials and discuss the children's existing knowledge about materials. The chart could also be used to record the results of a practical investigation.

Developing Literacy
Text Level Year 1
© A & C Black

Making charts: 2

- **Look at things people used at home a hundred years ago.**

Use information books.

- **Compare them with things people use today.**

- **Draw and write on the chart.**

A hundred years ago	Today
a flat iron	an electric iron

Now try this!

- **Make a chart about toys a hundred years ago and toys today.**

Use information books.

Teachers' note Provide reference books about Victorian homes (or provide and discuss artefacts such as a stone hot-water bottle, a dolly tub, a washboard, a mangle, an iron kettle and a carpet-beater). For the extension activity provide reference books about Victorian toys or examples of the real things.

Developing Literacy
Text Level Year 1
© A & C Black

Beach report

• **Look at the picture.**

• **Fill in the gaps.**

The children are at the _____.

They have made a _____.

There are _____ on the sandcastle.

There is _____ around the sandcastle.

• **Write two other sentences about**

the sandcastle.

_____

_____

_____

_____

Teachers' note Before the children begin the activity read the words in the word-bank with them
and explain any they do not understand. You could ask them to take turns to give a sentence to
build up a description of the picture.

Developing Literacy
Text Level Year 1
© A & C Black

• **Read about the horse.**

The horse has four legs.
It walks or runs on all
four legs. It has hair all
over its skin. The horse
has hard feet called hooves.
It has a tail made of hair.

• **Fill in the factfile.**

Animal _____

Number of legs _____

How it moves _____

_____

Skin _____

Feet _____

Tail _____

Picture

Now try this!

• **Make a factfile about another animal.**

Use information books.

Teachers' note With the children, read the description of the horse. For the extension activity provide reference books about animals and remind the children how to use the contents page and index to find the information they need.

Developing Literacy
Text Level Year 1
© A & C Black

Planning a non-fiction book

The children are making a book about their school.

• Read what they say.

We need a title page...

...a page about the grounds...

...and a page about our class.

...a contents page...

...a page about the teachers...

...a page about the building...

• Write a heading for each page.

Page 1	Page 2	Page 3
Page 4	Page 5	Page 6

• Write the title page and the contents page.

Teachers' note With the children, read the speech bubbles; model with them how to turn the children's words into page titles.

Developing Literacy
Text Level Year 1
© A & C Black